Design Thinking

Design Thinking

Revolutionize Your Approach to Problem-Solving

B. Vincent

QuantumQuill Press

CONTENTS

1

Introduction to Design Thinking

Definition and Outline

Configuration Believing is a critical thinking approach that underlines figuring out the client's necessities, testing suspicions, and reclassifying issues trying to distinguish elective techniques and arrangements that probably won't be in a split second obvious with our underlying degree of understanding. At its center, Plan Figuring looks to reveal imaginative arrangements by moving toward issues according to the client's point of view, in this way joining sympathy for the setting of an issue, innovativeness in the age of experiences and arrangements, and sanity in dissecting and fitting answers for the specific circumstance.

Dissimilar to conventional critical thinking strategies that start with a reasonable issue and look for the most productive arrangement, Plan Figuring begins with the acknowledgment that the actual issue probably won't be completely perceived. This technique energizes scrutinizing the issue, the suppositions behind it, and the ramifications of expected arrangements. An iterative cycle includes understanding the human necessities included, re-outlining the issue in human-driven ways, making a large number of thoughts in meetings to generate new ideas, taking on an active methodology in prototyping, and fostering a testable model. Really at that time do the arrangements start to arise and are retested and adjusted until the right arrangement is recognized.

This human-focused way to deal with development incorporates the necessities of individuals, the potential outcomes of innovation, and the prerequisites for business achievement. It assists associations in different areas with accomplishing advancement arrangements that are profoundly human in nature.

Authentic Setting and Development

The underlying foundations of Configuration Thinking can be followed back to the 1960s and 70s, where it started to come to fruition as a conventional technique. At first, it was firmly connected with modern plan and the improvement of items that were both practical and stylishly engaging. After some time, be that as it may, its pertinence has expanded fundamentally, enveloping administrations, cycles, and even frameworks for complex issues across many disciplines.

Herbert Simon's 1969 original work, "The Studies of the Fake," is frequently credited with laying the central hypothesis behind Plan Thinking. Simon suggested that plan ought to be viewed as a science by its own doing — one that concentrates on the counterfeit world we make. His thoughts enlivened another age of masterminds to investigate how plan standards could be applied to tackle item plan issues as well as intricate cultural and business challenges.

During the 1980s and 90s, Plan Believing was additionally advocated by configuration firms like IDEO and foundations, for example, the Stanford d.school. They developed the training from an item configuration concentration to a more extensive critical thinking instrument. This period saw the crystallization of the cycle into additional organized stages, making it more open and material to a more extensive scope of issues.

Significance In this day and age

In the present quick moving, innovation driven world, the difficulties we face are more perplexing and interconnected than any other time. Conventional straight critical thinking techniques are much of the time deficient while managing these multi-layered issues. Configuration Figuring offers a method for exploring this intricacy by zeroing in on grasping human requirements and ways of behaving, empowering unique reasoning, and cultivating a culture of trial and error and prototyping.

The significance of Configuration Figuring in this day and age couldn't possibly be more significant. It isn't simply a pattern; it is a reaction to the rising intricacy of our general surroundings. In business, it assists organizations with creating items and administrations that profoundly resound with clients. In training, it empowers decisive reasoning and imagination among understudies. In friendly development, it gives a structure to creating arrangements that are both effective and reasonable.

Besides, Plan Thinking encourages a mentality of sympathy, cooperation, and confidence. It enables people and groups to move toward difficulties with a feeling of probability as opposed to limitation.

The Five Phases of Design Thinking

Understand: Your Crowd

The main stage, Identify, the establishment whereupon the whole Plan Thinking process is fabricated. It includes figuring out the requirements, inspirations, and ways of behaving of individuals you're planning for. This profound plunge into the client's reality is vital for creating experiences that lead to inventive arrangements.

Compassion in Plan Thinking goes past simple perception; it requires drenching, commitment, and undivided attention. Procedures, for example, ethnographic field studies, client meetings, and persona advancement are utilized to assemble rich bits of knowledge. These techniques assist planners with venturing into the shoes of their clients, grasping their encounters from a profoundly private viewpoint.

The objective of the Relate isn't simply to gather information however to feel what your clients feel. Thusly, fashioners can distinguish idle requirements and wants that clients themselves may not know about. This stage difficulties suspicions and inclinations, opening up new roads for development.

Understanding not a one-time task however a constant cycle that illuminates all phases of Configuration Thinking. It guarantees that the arrangements created are actually practical as well as profoundly resounding with the ideal interest group.

Characterize: Outlining the Issue

With a profound comprehension of the client's necessities and difficulties, the Characterize stage centers around outlining the right issue to settle. This includes orchestrating the accumulated bits of knowledge into an unmistakable, noteworthy issue explanation that directs the remainder of the plan cycle.

A clear cut issue proclamation is client driven, featuring explicit necessities and experiences. It goes about as a compass, keeping the group adjusted and zeroed in on the main thing to the client. Strategies, for example, "How should we" questions work with the change from bits of knowledge to significant issue proclamations, empowering an expansive investigation of likely arrangements.

The Characterize stage is basic since it sets the course for ideation. By obviously articulating the issue, planners guarantee that their innovative endeavors are focused on and pertinent. This stage requires decisive reasoning and insight to distil complex client information into a brief issue explanation that epitomizes the quintessence of the test.

Ideate: Producing Intelligent fixes

Ideation is the stage where imagination and development become the dominant focal point. With an unmistakable issue explanation close by, fashioners conceptualize a large number of thoughts, regardless of how stunning they might appear. The objective is to produce an enormous amount of thoughts, encouraging a culture of imagination and liberality.

Strategies like meetings to generate new ideas, Hurry, and psyche planning are utilized to energize different reasoning. This stage benefits from variety, as fluctuated points of view lead to more extravagant, more inventive arrangements. It's a cooperative exertion where judgment is suspended, and each thought is invited and esteemed.

The Ideate stage is where the imperatives of the truth are briefly saved, taking into account the investigation of the limits of innovativeness and development. It's a urgent second in the Plan Thinking process, as it lays the preparation for the substantial signs of arrangements in the ensuing stages.

Model: Building Unmistakable Portrayals

Prototyping is the stage where thoughts are changed into unmistakable portrayals. These models can go from straightforward paper models to additional modern computerized or actual manifestations. The design is to rejuvenate thoughts in a structure that can be communicated with, tried, and refined.

Prototyping is iterative; every variant tries to address explicit inquiries and test speculations about the arrangement. It's an involved stage where disappointment is viewed as a significant wellspring of learning. By making thoughts unmistakable, planners can distinguish unanticipated issues and assemble substantial input from clients.

This stage demystifies and democratizes the plan interaction. Models make thoughts open, taking into consideration coordinated effort and criticism from clients as well as from cross-disciplinary colleagues. It's a basic move toward making dynamic ideas concrete and noteworthy.

Test: Refining Your Answers

The last stage, Test, includes placing the models in the possession of clients to accumulate criticism and experiences. This stage is tied in with realizing what works, what doesn't, and why. Testing is definitely not an oddball occasion however a repetitive cycle that feeds once more into the prior stages, considering refinement and emphasis.

Client criticism during the Test stage is priceless. It gives a rude awakening and guarantees that the arrangement resolves the issue as well as does as such in a manner that is significant and effective to the client. Strategies, for example, A/B testing, ease of use testing, and in-setting perception are utilized to accumulate this criticism.

Testing highlights the iterative idea of Configuration Thinking. It's tied in with refining thoughts, gaining from client collaborations, and consistently working on the arrangement. This stage guarantees that the eventual outcome or administration isn't simply a hypothetical development yet a viable, client focused arrangement that has a genuine effect in individuals' lives.

Empathizing with Your Users

Understanding the Substance of Sympathy in Plan Thinking

Compassion goes past simple compassion or grasping; it's tied in with venturing into the shoes of others, seeing the world according to their viewpoint, and feeling what they feel. With regards to Configuration Thinking, sympathy empowers fashioners to uncover the profound, frequently unsaid necessities of those they are planning for. This sympathetic knowledge drives genuinely imaginative arrangements that resound on a human level.

The most common way of relating noticing, connecting with, and drenching oneself in the clients' encounters. It's tied in with being open, inquisitive, and suspending one's own convictions and predispositions to comprehend someone else's viewpoint genuinely. This doesn't simply apply to individual clients yet stretches out to figuring out the more extensive setting of their lives, including the social, social, and actual conditions in which they live and communicate.

Strategies for Compassion

A few techniques work with compassion, each offering an alternate focal point through which to figure out clients:

•Ethnographic Field Studies: This includes noticing clients right at home, furnishing experiences into how they collaborate with their reality and the items or administrations inside it. It's tied in with catching their ways of behaving, schedules, and ceremonies in setting.

•Client Meetings: Directed with an emphasis on narrating, these meetings urge clients to share their encounters, inspirations, and difficulties. The point is to investigate the profound and mental underpinnings of their ways of behaving and choices.

•Persona Improvement: Making point by point profiles of original clients, known as personas, assists with solidifying the bits of knowledge accumulated from perceptions and meetings. Personas make the theoretical idea of a "client" concrete, directing the plan cycle by keeping the group zeroed in on client driven arrangements.

•Compassion Planning: This visual instrument catches what clients say, think, do, and feel, offering an all encompassing perspective on their experience. A cooperative activity distils perceptions into experiences, assisting with making a mutual perspective among the plan group.

•Client Excursion Planning: This procedure includes graphing the client's excursion with an item or administration, distinguishing all the touchpoints where they cooperate with it. It features areas of grating and pleasure, giving a guide to upgrading the general client experience.

Stories from the Field: Instances of Compassion in real life

Certifiable models rejuvenate the force of sympathy in driving development:

•Medical care: A clinical gadget organization utilized ethnographic exploration to grasp the everyday difficulties of diabetes patients. By carrying on with a typical day for their clients, creators fostered another insulin siphon that was more instinctive as well as more incorporated into the patients' ways of life, fundamentally decreasing the disgrace and burden related with diabetes the executives.

•Training: An ed-tech startup led profound plunge interviews with the two instructors and understudies to figure out their dissatisfactions with existing learning stages. Experiences from these meetings prompted the improvement of an adaptable learning stage that tended to the particular necessities of various learning styles, making instruction more open and connecting with for a different understudy body.

•Monetary Administrations: A bank utilized sympathy planning to uncover the tensions and goals of first-time home purchasers. This grasping prompted the formation of another set-up of administrations that directed clients through the home purchasing process, making it not so much overwhelming but rather more straightforward.

Activities to Upgrade Sympathetic Comprehension

Building compassion is an expertise that can be created through training. Here are a few activities intended to upgrade sympathetic comprehension:

•Shadowing: Go through a day shadowing a client, noticing their schedules and communications without obstruction. This vivid experience gives profound bits of knowledge into the client's reality.

•Pretending: Assume the job of a client exploring a particular situation or challenge. This exercise assists with assimilating the client's feelings and viewpoints.

•Client Journal Studies: Urge clients to keep a journal of their encounters with an item or administration. Investigating these journals can uncover experiences into clients' necessities and disappointments after some time.

•Sympathy Studios: Put together studios where colleagues share their bits of knowledge and encounters from compassion works out.

These meetings encourage a culture of compassion and coordinated effort, guaranteeing that client centricity stays at the core of the plan interaction.

Relating to clients is in excess of a stage in the Plan Thinking process; a mentality saturates each part of plan. It moves planners to look past the self-evident, to reveal the implicit requirements and wants that drive really extraordinary arrangements. As we continue to the Characterize stage, the experiences acquired from identifying guide the outlining of issues in a manner that lines up with the clients' genuine requirements and goals, making way for imaginative, human-focused arrangements.

4 |

Defining Your Problem Space

The Specialty of Issue Definition in Plan Thinking

Characterizing the issue is a craftsmanship that includes refining the complex, frequently chaotic bits of knowledge accumulated during the Understand into a sound, centered issue proclamation. This assertion fills in as a north star, directing the ideation and improvement processes. A distinct issue explanation is explicit, human-focused, and sufficiently wide to consider artistic liberty yet thin to the point of being sensible.

Instruments for Powerful Issue Definition

A few devices and strategies aid this basic stage, empowering groups to progress from wide perceptions to explicit issue proclamations:

•Fondness Graphs: This device helps in coordinating and sorting the perceptions and experiences from the Sympathize. By gathering related bits of knowledge, examples and subjects arise, featuring the center issues that need tending to.

•Perspective (POV) Explanations: A POV proclamation explains the issue according to the client's point of view, zeroing in on unambiguous necessities and experiences. It's a reexamining device that moves the concentration from a general issue to a customized, noteworthy test.

•How Should We (HMW) Questions: Changing POV articulations into HMW questions opens up the issue space for innovative investigation. These inquiries are purposefully hopeful, welcoming a large number of arrangements.

•5 Whys: This strategy includes inquiring "Why?" multiple times to strip away the layers of side effects and arrive at the hidden reason for an issue. It guarantees that the characterized issue tends to the underlying driver as opposed to only the surface issues.

Contextual investigations: Effective Issue Outlining

Looking at effective uses of issue outlining can enlighten the extraordinary force of a distinct issue space:

•Innovation Area: A main tech organization utilized proclivity outlines to blend client criticism on their product's convenience. The subsequent POV proclamation zeroed in on the requirement for a more natural connection point, prompting an upgrade that fundamentally superior client commitment and fulfillment.

•Social Advancement: A non-benefit association tending to water shortage in emerging nations reevaluated their concern through HMW questions. Rather than zeroing in on the absence of water, they inquired, "How should we enable networks to deal with their water assets economically?" This redefinition prompted the advancement of local area drove water preservation programs that were both compelling and maintainable.

•Purchaser Items: A food and drink organization utilized the 5 Whys strategy to comprehend declining deals of a famous item. The issue was at first remembered to be about taste, however the underlying driver was distinguished as a bundling issue that made the item challenging to utilize. An update of the bundling switched the deals decline.

Studio Thoughts for Issue Definition

Working with studios can be a viable method for drawing in groups in the issue definition process. Here are a few thoughts for studios that empower joint effort and imagination:

•Understanding Sharing Meetings: Begin with a meeting where each colleague shares a vital knowledge from the Relate. This aggregate sharing can uncover new points of view and extend the's comprehension group might interpret the issue space.

•POV Frantic Libs: Utilize a format to assist groups with making POV explanations. For instance, "[(User)] needs [(need)] on the grounds that [(insight)]." This fun loving methodology can demystify the interaction and flash imaginative reasoning.

•HMW Conceptualizing: Break into little gatherings and create however many HMW questions as could be allowed from the characterized POV explanations. This exercise energizes expansive reasoning and guarantees that no potential trouble spot is disregarded.

Beating Difficulties in Issue Definition

Characterizing the issue space is much of the time testing, yet certain systems can assist with defeating normal traps:

•Keep away from Arrangement Predisposition: Remain fixed on the issue instead of leaping to arrangements. Untimely intermingling on an answer can daze you to elective, possibly more creative ways.

•Embrace Vagueness: The Characterize stage frequently includes exploring vulnerability. Embrace this equivocalness as a wellspring of inventiveness as opposed to a boundary to advance.

•Emphasize on Definitions: Issue explanations are yet to be determined. Return to and refine your concern definition as new bits of knowledge arise.

Characterizing the issue space in Plan Believing is about clearness, concentration, and compassion. It changes crude, sympathetic bits of knowledge into an unmistakable heading for development, making way for the imaginative investigation in the Ideate stage. As we continue, recollect that the strength of the arrangements you create is straightforwardly attached to the lucidity and profundity of the issue you've characterized. With a very much expressed issue proclamation as our aide, we're presently ready to investigate the tremendous scene of likely arrangements in the Ideate stage.

5

Ideation: The Heart of Innovation

Releasing Innovativeness

Ideation is the stage where innovativeness becomes the over-whelming focus. It's an encouragement to think extensively, to challenge existing suspicions, and to investigate new domains without the apprehension about committing errors. The objective is to produce a different pool of thoughts, from the gradual to the progressive, that address the characterized issue space in original ways.

Methods for Ideation

To saddle the innovative capability of groups, an assortment of ideation procedures are utilized. Every strategy offers a remarkable pathway to development, empowering various methods of reasoning and coordinated effort:

•Conceptualizing: The most broadly perceived ideation procedure, conceptualizing is a gathering movement pointed toward creating a huge amount of thoughts in a brief period. The accentuation is on amount over quality, with all decisions suspended to support free-streaming innovativeness.

•Hurry: An abbreviation for Substitute, Join, Adjust, Change, Put to another utilization, Dispose of, and Switch, Rush is an agenda based procedure that prompts members to contemplate an issue or an item in various ways. It's especially powerful for developing existing arrangements into something new and inventive.

•Mind Planning: This method includes making a visual portrayal of thoughts around a focal topic. It empowers acquainted thinking, making it simpler to see the associations between various considerations and ideas.

•Drawing and Storyboarding: These visual procedures consider the quick investigation of thoughts and situations. They make conceptual ideas substantial, working with better comprehension and correspondence inside the group.

•Pretending: Carrying on situations can reveal bits of knowledge into the client experience and expected arrangements. It's a strong method for feeling for clients and to investigate the common sense and effect of various thoughts.

•Six Reasoning Caps: Created by Edward de Bono, this strategy energizes taking a gander at issues according to six particular points of view (close to home, instructive, consistent, innovative, basic, and hopeful). It guarantees a more adjusted investigation of thoughts.

The Force of Disparate and United Thinking

Ideation wavers among dissimilar and concurrent reasoning. Different reasoning is tied in with producing however many thoughts as could be allowed, empowering nonlinear reasoning and investigation. Concurrent reasoning, then again, limits these thoughts into achievable arrangements. Adjusting these two methods of reasoning is vital for powerful ideation.

True Instances of Compelling Ideation

•A Tech Goliath's Development Lab: In their mission to reclassify home diversion, a group utilized outlining and storyboarding to ideate around the client experience. This prompted the advancement of an intelligent home framework that consistently incorporates with day to day existence, changing the idea of savvy homes.

•Social Effect Configuration Firm: By utilizing the Hurry method, a firm devoted to further developing admittance to clean water in far off regions changed their way to deal with water refinement, bringing about a convenient, easy to use water filtration gadget that radically superior convenience and reception.

•Instructive Toy Organization: Through pretending, the organization dove into the personalities of kids, prompting the ideation of a progression of instructive toys that mix learning with play in creative ways, changing their product offering.

Working with Viable Ideation Meetings

To boost the result of ideation meetings, certain practices can improve innovativeness and cooperation:

•Establish an Open Climate: Encourage a space where all thoughts are invited, and members have a real sense of reassurance to share unafraid of judgment.

•Empower Wild Thoughts: Some of the time, the most shocking thoughts make ready for the most creative arrangements. Empower thinking past the typical limits.

•Expand on Others' Thoughts: Ideation is a cooperative interaction. Expanding on the thoughts of others can prompt unforeseen and creative arrangements.

•Utilize Visual Guides: Visuals can animate creative mind and assist with explaining complex thoughts, making them a useful asset in ideation meetings.

Difficulties and Arrangements in Ideation

While ideation is an innovative and invigorating stage, it accompanies its arrangement of difficulties:

•Thought Over-burden: The wealth of thoughts can overpower. Utilizing models to focus on thoughts for additional investigation can assist with dealing with this over-burden.

•Congruity Tension: Groups could float towards more secure, more natural thoughts. Empowering risk-taking and esteeming all commitments can moderate this tension.

•Investigation Loss of motion: A lot of examination can smother innovativeness. Setting clear time limits for ideation meetings can keep the energy high and the thoughts streaming.

Ideation is the powerful center of the Plan Thinking process, a stage that requests receptiveness, inventiveness, and joint effort. It's where the seeds of advancement are planted, fit to be refined and acknowledged in the Prototyping stage. As we push ahead, recollect that each noteworthy arrangement begins as a simple thought, a chance investigated in the rich grounds of the Ideate stage.

6

Prototyping as a Learning Tool

The Quintessence of Prototyping

Prototyping is the epitome of the "bomb quick, catch on quickly" reasoning. It's tied in with rejuvenating thoughts in the speediest, generally effective way that is available to test suppositions and accumulate experiences. Models can go from basic portrays or paper models to more modern computerized or physical mockups. The key is that they are speedy and modest to make, taking into account fast cycle and learning.

Sorts of Models

Understanding the various levels and reasons for models is significant for really utilizing them as learning devices:

•Low-Loyalty Models: These are no fuss adaptations of thoughts, frequently produced using straightforward materials like paper, cardboard, or essential computerized mockups. Their motivation is to test and refine the center ideas of a plan.

•High-Constancy Models: These are more refined and intently look like the end result, including usefulness and appearance. High-devotion models are utilized to test convenience and assemble point by point criticism.

•Computerized Models: Made with programming devices, advanced models can reenact UIs and connections. They are especially helpful for testing programming applications and advanced administrations.

•Actual Models: These are unmistakable models of items that clients can interface with. Actual models are fundamental for testing the ergonomics, materials, and ease of use of actual items.

Prototyping Strategies and Devices

Various strategies and devices can be utilized to make models, each fit to various phases of the plan cycle and kinds of items:

•Outlining and Storyboarding: Speedy and powerful for beginning phase ideation, considering the quick investigation of ideas and client situations.

•Paper Prototyping: Ideal for testing UIs and work processes without the requirement for any advanced turn of events.

•3D Printing: Offers the capacity to make definite actual models that clients can associate with, making it priceless for testing structure and capability in actual items.

•Computerized Mockup Instruments: Programming like Sketch, Adobe XD, and Figma permits originators to make high-devotion advanced models that reproduce client collaborations with programming and advanced items.

•Equipment Prototyping: Apparatuses like Arduino and Raspberry Pi empower the making of models for electronic and shrewd gadgets, considering the testing of functionalities and client communications.

Genuine Utilizations of Prototyping

•Purchaser Hardware Organization: Utilized 3D printing to make actual models of another wearable gadget. This permitted the group to test the solace, fit, and convenience, prompting a few emphasess that fundamentally better the eventual outcome.

•Programming Startup: Utilized computerized prototyping devices to quickly repeat on the plan of a versatile application, testing client streams and points of interaction to upgrade convenience and client commitment.

•Instructive Toys Maker: Made paper and actual models of another instructive toy, empowering early testing with youngsters to notice connection examples and learning results, which educated the advancement regarding the eventual outcome.

Techniques for Viable Prototyping

To use prototyping as a strong learning instrument, think about the accompanying techniques:

•Model Early and Frequently: The sooner you begin prototyping, the sooner you can start learning and repeating. Try not to hang tight for a "great" thought; model to test and refine your ideas.

•Embrace Disappointment as a Learning A valuable open door: Every model is a theory being tried. Gain from what doesn't fill in as much as from what does, and utilize these experiences to illuminate your next emphasis.

•Center around Key Inquiries: Every model ought to mean to respond to explicit inquiries. Be clear about the thing you're trying with every emphasis to guarantee centered learning.

•Include Clients Early: Get models under the control of clients quickly. Their criticism is priceless for approving presumptions and revealing new experiences.

•Repeat In light of Criticism: Utilize the input from each prototyping round to refine and work on your plan. Keep in mind, prototyping is an iterative cycle where each cycle carries you more like an answer that addresses clients' issues.

Prototyping isn't just about making items; it's tied in with learning and developing thoughts in a substantial configuration. It's an iterative course of investigation, testing, and refinement that carries clearness to the plan cycle and guarantees that the last arrangements are grounded in genuine client needs and bits of knowledge. As we move into the Testing stage, these models will go through thorough assessment, further refining the answers for meet the clients' actual necessities.

7

Implementing Design Thinking in Business and Product Development

In the business world, Plan Believing is saddled to enhance items, administrations, and cycles. A methodology moves past conventional plans of action, zeroing in rather on client necessities to make seriously captivating, successful, and cutthroat contributions.

•Client Experience Upgrade: Organizations use Configuration Remembering to outline client travels and update touchpoints for further developed fulfillment and steadfastness.

•Item Advancement: Organizations utilize iterative prototyping and testing to foster new items that better address client issues and assumptions.

•Process Overhaul: Associations apply Configuration Remembering to smooth out tasks, making them more productive and easy to use for the two clients and representatives.

Model: A main innovation organization could utilize Configuration Remembering to create a new cell phone. By identifying with clients, they find an interest for more natural protection controls. Through iterative plan and testing, they foster an exceptional connection point that tends to this need, separating their item in a packed market.

Configuration Thinking in Training and Learning

Schooling systems are progressively taking on Plan Remembering to encourage a seriously captivating, important, and creative learning climate. It advances decisive reasoning, innovativeness, and joint effort among understudies and instructors.

•Educational program Configuration: Plan Believing is utilized to foster educational programs that are more lined up with understudies' true requirements and interests, making learning seriously captivating and relevant.

•Instructive Apparatuses and Innovations: Instructors and fashioners team up to make devices and advancements that improve growth opportunities, in light of profound comprehension of understudies' difficulties and requirements.

•Learning Spaces: Schools and colleges are reconsidering physical and virtual learning conditions to cultivate cooperation, imagination, and inclusivity, utilizing bits of knowledge got from the identify.

Model: An instructive foundation might utilize Configuration Remembering to update its web based learning stage. By profoundly understanding the difficulties and requirements of understudies and instructors, the foundation makes a more instinctive, open, and co-operative internet learning climate.

Configuration Thinking for Social Development and Local area Tasks

Configuration Thinking offers useful assets for tending to complex social difficulties, advancing reasonable arrangements that are well established in the networks they serve.

•Local area Commitment: By relating to local area individuals, social trend-setters can distinguish squeezing necessities and co-make arrangements that have certifiable purchase in and pertinence.

•Public Administrations: Legislatures and NGOs use Configuration Remembering to overhaul public administrations, making them more open, effective, and easy to use.

•Natural Maintainability: Associations apply Configuration Remembering to foster imaginative ways to deal with supportability, making arrangements that offset human necessities with ecological protection.

Model: A non-benefit association could utilize Configuration Remembering to handle metropolitan food deserts. By understanding the local area's requirements, the association co-plans an organization of metropolitan nurseries and portable food markets, giving new produce and drawing locally in feasible practices.

Beating Difficulties in Executing Configuration Thinking

While Configuration Figuring offers various advantages, its execution can confront difficulties:

•Social Opposition: Associations acquainted with customary various leveled and departmental designs might oppose the cooperative, iterative nature of Configuration Thinking.

•Asset Limitations: The time and assets expected for careful examination, prototyping, and testing can be a boundary, especially in high speed or asset lashed conditions.

•Scaling Arrangements: Plan Thinking can prompt inventive arrangements on a limited scale, yet scaling these answers for a more extensive crowd or setting can challenge.

Procedures for Progress:

•Cultivate a Culture of Development: Empower a hierarchical culture that values inventiveness, trial and error, and client centricity.

•Accentuate Speedy Successes: Begin with little, sensible activities that exhibit the worth of Configuration Thinking, gathering speed and purchase in.

•Work together Across Limits: Separate storehouses inside associations and urge interdisciplinary groups to use assorted points of view.

Configuration Thinking's materialness across different settings highlights its comprehensiveness and viability as a critical thinking approach. From improving business intensity to changing school systems and handling social difficulties, Plan Figuring enables associations and networks to foster arrangements that are creative, human-focused, and significant. As this philosophy keeps on advancing, its capability to drive positive change across areas stays immense and to a great extent undiscovered. By embracing compassion, coordinated effort, and iterative learning, we can use Configuration Remembering to address probably the most squeezing difficulties within recent memory, making a more comprehensive, supportable, and imaginative future.

8

Identifying Common Challenges in Design Thinking

Protection from Change

One of the main boundaries to carrying out Plan Believing is protection from change. Associations acquainted with customary, straight ways to deal with critical thinking might find the iterative, non-direct course of Configuration Thinking testing. This obstruction can come from an apprehension about the obscure, an absence of comprehension of the procedure, or saw dangers to laid out power designs and jobs.

Combination into Corporate Culture

Configuration Thinking requires a culture of development, co-operation, and an eagerness to embrace disappointment as a learning a valuable open door. Developing such a culture in conditions where disappointment is seen adversely, or where divisions work in storehouses, can especially challenge.

Asset Limitations

The iterative idea of Configuration Thinking, with its accentuation on continued prototyping and testing, can be asset concentrated.

Associations might battle with allotting adequate time, work force, and financial plan to completely uphold the interaction.

Versatility of Arrangements

Configuration Thinking can prompt imaginative arrangements on a limited scale or inside unambiguous undertaking boundaries. Notwithstanding, scaling these answers for a more extensive setting or coordinating them into existing frameworks and cycles can introduce huge difficulties.

Techniques for Conquering Difficulties

Encouraging Hierarchical Purchase In

•Teach and Backer: Start by instructing partners about the worth of Configuration Thinking, utilizing contextual analyses and proof of its progress in different businesses.

•Exhibit Fast Wins: Execute Configuration Figuring on limited scope projects that can rapidly show results, gathering speed and backing for more extensive reception.

Developing a Culture of Advancement

•Show others how its done: Administration ought to effectively partake in and support Configuration Thinking projects, flagging its significance to the association.

•Observe Gaining from Disappointment: Make a place of refuge for trial and error, where disappointment is viewed as an essential step towards development. Featuring and gaining from projects that didn't go as arranged can support this.

Overseeing Assets Actually

•Staged Approach: Begin with low-devotion models and limited scope tests to limit asset utilization. Slowly increment venture as arrangements demonstrate their worth.

•Influence Cross-Practical Groups: Use the different abilities and points of view inside the association to improve the Plan Thinking process, spreading the responsibility and cultivating a feeling of pride across divisions.

Guaranteeing Versatility

•Plan for Scale Early: Consider versatility from the very beginning of the Plan Thinking process, expecting the difficulties of more extensive execution.

•Emphasize Past the Arrangement: Utilize the standards of Configuration Remembering to address the difficulties of scaling arrangements. This could include repeating on plans of action, circulation channels, or client assistance frameworks to help the new arrangement.

Genuine Models

•A Global Company defeated protection from Configuration Thinking by starting a progression of studios where chiefs partook in sympathy practices and prototyping meetings. Seeing the system in real life, joined with accounts of fruitful executions, helped shift discernments and encourage chief purchase in.

•A Tech Startup battling with asset requirements embraced a staged way to deal with Configuration Thinking. By zeroing in on fast, low-loyalty prototyping and utilizing client criticism from beginning phases, they had the option to repeat rapidly without significant venture, slowly scaling their answer as trust in its feasibility developed.

•An Instructive Foundation tended to versatility by making arrangements for it all along. They fostered an experimental run program utilizing Configuration Remembering to overhaul a course. The pilot's prosperity gave an outline to scaling the methodology across the educational plan, upheld by ceaseless criticism and emphasis.

Beating the difficulties related with Configuration Thinking requires an essential methodology zeroed in on schooling, social change, and asset the board. By encouraging hierarchical purchase in, developing a culture that embraces development and disappointment, overseeing assets carefully, and making arrangements for versatility, associations can open the maximum capacity of Configuration Thinking. These procedures alleviate the hindrances as well as improve the general adequacy and effect of Configuration Thinking projects. Eventually, the way to exploring these difficulties lies in embracing the very standards at the core of Configuration Thinking: sympathy, joint effort, and iterative learning.

9 |

Emerging Trends and Technologies

Coordination with Trend setting innovations: The combination of Configuration Thinking with state of the art advances like man-made consciousness (simulated intelligence), AI, and the Web of Things (IoT) is set to extend. This intermingling will empower more complex comprehension of client needs and ways of behaving, prompting developments that are mechanically cutting-edge as well as profoundly human-focused.

Manageability and Social Advancement: As worldwide difficulties, for example, environmental change and social imbalance escalate, Plan Thinking will progressively be applied to foster supportable arrangements and advance social development. Its compassionate and iterative nature makes it appropriate to handling complex issues that require a profound comprehension of different viewpoints and necessities.

Virtual Cooperation: The ascent of remote work and virtual coordinated effort instruments presents the two difficulties and open doors for Configuration Thinking. Future cycles of the cycle will probably use computer generated reality (VR), expanded reality

(AR), and other computerized coordinated effort devices to work with sympathy works out, prototyping, and testing in a disseminated climate.

Growing Degree and Reach

More extensive Reception Across Areas: Plan Believing is set to grow past its conventional fortresses in business and item improvement into areas like government, training, and medical services. This more extensive reception will be driven by a developing acknowledgment of the worth of client focused plan in tending to complex difficulties.

Schooling and Preparing: As the interest for Configuration Thinking abilities develops, so too will the accentuation on schooling and preparing around here. We can hope to see Configuration Thinking standards coordinated into educational plans across levels of schooling, as well as in proficient turn of events and corporate preparation programs.

Worldwide and Social Transformation: Plan Thinking will keep on adjusting to various social settings and worldwide difficulties, turning out to be more comprehensive and intelligent of assorted points of view. This development will advance the approach, making it much more flexible and successful.

The fate of Configuration Believing is energetic and promising. Its standards of compassion, coordinated effort, and iterative learning are immortal and general, offering a strong structure for development in an undeniably perplexing world. As we embrace new advancements and face worldwide difficulties, Plan Thinking will develop, impacting and being affected by the world it tries to get to the next level. Its future will be described by extended applications, more profound reconciliations with innovation, and a supported spotlight on human-driven arrangements. By remaining consistent with its center standards while adjusting to the evolving scene, Plan

Believing will keep on being a crucial instrument for development, equipped for tending to probably the most squeezing difficulties within recent memory.

| 34 |

The Future of Design Thinking

As we look toward the future, Plan Thinking remains at the slope of huge development. This development is pushed by the fast progressions in innovation, the moving elements of worldwide economies, and the steadily changing scene of cultural requirements. The versatility of Configuration Figuring makes it intrinsically future-verification, prepared to coordinate new apparatuses and answer arising difficulties.

Arising advances like computerized reasoning (simulated intelligence), augmented reality (VR), and the Web of Things (IoT) are growing the tool stash accessible for fashioners, offering better approaches to identify, and test. These innovations vow to extend how we might interpret client encounters, empowering the making of arrangements that are more customized and open. Besides, the developing accentuation on maintainability and moral plan pushes Configuration Remembering to integrate natural and social contemplations into each phase of the critical thinking process.

The democratization of Configuration Believing is another key pattern. As the technique turns out to be more far reaching, it's being embraced by a more extensive scope of disciplines past customary plan fields, from medical services and schooling to public strategy and then some. This cross-fertilization of thoughts and approaches enhances the Plan Thinking process, prompting more inventive and significant arrangements.

Moreover, the standards of Configuration Believing are being applied to handle foundational challenges, for example, environmental change, social imbalance, and the fate of work. This expansive application highlights the philosophy's flexibility and its capability to add to significant, fundamental change.

As we push ahead, the combination of Configuration Thinking with different techniques and the constant transformation to new difficulties will just improve its significance and adequacy. The eventual fate of Configuration Believing is one of extended limits, further effects, and proceeded with development.

End: Your Process Forward with Configuration Thinking

Setting out on an excursion with Configuration Believing is a promise to ceaseless learning, sympathy, and development. It is a mentality as much as a procedure, one that moves you to see past the self-evident, to grasp further necessities, and to make arrangements that genuinely have an effect.

As you push ahead, recall that Plan Believing is iterative. Each step, from relating to clients to testing and refining arrangements, is a chance for development and revelation. Embrace the non-straight nature of this interaction, and be ready to return again, rethink, and turn in light of what you realize.

The genuine force of Configuration Thinking lies in its human-focused approach. By keeping the necessities, wants, and encounters of individuals at the core of your work, you make more powerful arrangements as well as encourage a more comprehensive, feasible, and sympathetic world.

Whether you are a fashioner, instructor, business pioneer, or trend-setter, Plan Thinking offers a way to more profound comprehension and innovative critical thinking. The excursion forward isn't without its difficulties, however the prizes — groundbreaking arrangements, improved inventiveness, and the fulfillment of having a genuine effect — are endless.

As you proceed to investigate and apply Configuration Thinking, keep a receptive outlook, embrace sympathy, and forever gain from individuals and your general surroundings. Your excursion with Configuration Believing isn't just about the arrangements you make yet in addition about the experiences you gain and the distinction you make. Here's to your process forward, brimming with disclosure, advancement, and significant effect.

Appendix

Appendix A: Resources for Further Learning

1. Books:
    - "The Design of Everyday Things" by Don Norman
    - "Change by Design" by Tim Brown
    - "Design Thinking: Integrating Innovation, Customer Experience, and Brand Value" by Thomas Lockwood
2. Websites and Online Platforms:
    - IDEO.org (A global design consultancy that created a guide to Design Thinking)
    - Stanford d.school (Offers resources and guides on how to apply Design Thinking)
3. Courses and Workshops:
    - Introduction to Design Thinking (offered by Stanford d.school)
    - IDEO U's Design Thinking online courses

Appendix B: Templates and Tools

1. Empathy Map Template: A tool for synthesizing observations about a user's experience into actionable insights.
2. Persona Template: Helps in creating detailed profiles of typical users to guide the design process.
3. Customer Journey Map Template: For mapping the steps a customer goes through in engaging with a product or service, identifying key interactions and emotions.

4. How Might We (HMW) Question Template: A framework for transforming insights into open-ended questions that spur ideation.

Appendix C: Glossary of Terms

- Design Thinking: A user-centric approach to problem-solving that involves understanding the user's needs, ideating solutions, prototyping, and testing.
- Empathize: The first phase of Design Thinking, focused on understanding the needs, behaviors, and experiences of the users.
- Prototype: A simple model or draft version of a product or service used to explore or test ideas before final production.
- Iterative: A process characterized by repeated cycles of testing, learning, analyzing, and refining a product or service.
- User Persona: A semi-fictional character created to represent a user type that might use a service, product, site, or brand similarly.

Appendix D: Recommended Reading

1. Articles on the Future of Design Thinking:
   - Exploring how emerging technologies like AI and VR are integrating with Design Thinking to enhance user experience and innovation.
   - Discussions on the role of Design Thinking in addressing global challenges such as sustainability and social equity.
2. Case Studies:

◦ Detailed accounts of successful Design Thinking projects across industries, highlighting the process, challenges, and outcomes.

By providing these appendices, the book aims to equip readers with a comprehensive toolkit to navigate the complexities of Design Thinking, from foundational concepts to advanced applications. Whether you're a beginner eager to explore the potential of Design Thinking or a seasoned practitioner seeking to deepen your expertise, these resources offer valuable insights and practical tools to support your journey.

www.ingramcontent.com/pod-product-compliance
Lightning Source LLC
Chambersburg PA
CBHW031246130726
47988CB00008B/3265